D1468448

CONTENTS

The Fireside Book

A picture and a poem for every mood
chosen by

David Hope

Printed and published by D.C. THOMSON & CO., LTD.,
185 Fleet Street, LONDON EC4A 2HS. © D.C. Thomson & Co., Ltd., 2009

WINTER SNOWS

SNOWS of Winter
Swirling, drifting, settling,
Smoothing their way
Across the moor;
Lacing their way
Through the hedgerows,
The tangled undergrowth,
The criss-cross branches;
Catching the glint of sun
In diamond patterns . . .
Nature presents
Its seasonal gift . . .

Elizabeth Gozney

FALLING STARS

HOW many stars have softly slipped
  from Heaven's gentle, knowing grasp,
falling, landing, bodies tipped,
to slumber in the darkened grass?

How many stars have kissed the trees
with gold and diamond-spangled dust
as they tumbled through the leaves
in graceful arcs as all stars must?

I wonder when I wander there,
through timeless forests still and deep,
if I am walking unaware
upon the dreams of stars that sleep.

Rachel Wallace-Oberle

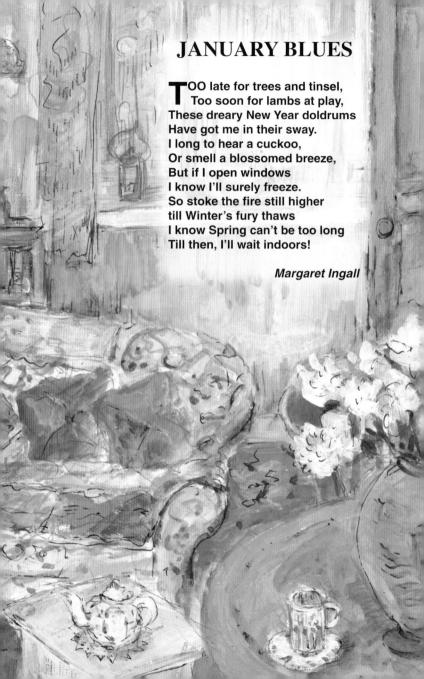

JANUARY BLUES

TOO late for trees and tinsel,
  Too soon for lambs at play,
These dreary New Year doldrums
Have got me in their sway.
I long to hear a cuckoo,
Or smell a blossomed breeze,
But if I open windows
I know I'll surely freeze.
So stoke the fire still higher
till Winter's fury thaws
I know Spring can't be too long
Till then, I'll wait indoors!

Margaret Ingall

SONG THRUSH

A CRYSTAL clear, triple note song,
   Repeating, cascading optimism
From the ash tree top,
Brim-filled with buds.

Chestnut speckled, bright breast
Feathers, puffing out,
Facing the chill
January wind.

On this day of mist and frost
The happy heart fills his soul
With an exuberance,
Simple, plain, defined.

How good it is
To breathe and sing,
How good
To be alive.

David Elder

TREAD SOFTLY

TREAD softly,
before the rumble of time.

Savour dawn's sweetness,
and feel the chill of Winter
as he limps away.

Spring whispers in the swirling light;
"See, I bring you new hope and life;
and on a dewy bud, a sign.
A flicker of Nature's wine

as April sings on earth again."

Mo Crawshaw

VOICE OF SPRING

STEPPING out in that hour before dawn
When the heavens revealed
Only their brightest stars,
I walked the beech wood,
Hearing, then stopping, listening
To crescendo sounds
Of birdsong multiply, intensify.
Blackbirds fluted notes in cadence,
Ascended, descended scales of gold;
A tiny wren bellowed a riposte,
High-pitched, concentrated;
Then a robin puffed out his chest
And pierced the frosted air
With a passionate voice of Spring.

David Elder

APRIL FROST

SUCH a cruel blow,
this late, unseasonal snow,
that brings an April frost
and lays the garden low.
Will all be lost?

Or will weather relent
to save the flowering currant
and the daffodils lying
heavy and aslant
with snow, frozen, dying?

It does indeed!
As if by Heaven decreed,
next morning's sun
kisses the almost dead,
secures their resurrection.

Snow loosens its grip,
and from the frail cowslip,
freed from frost,
tears of plant-joy drip.
Not a single flower is lost!

John Ellis

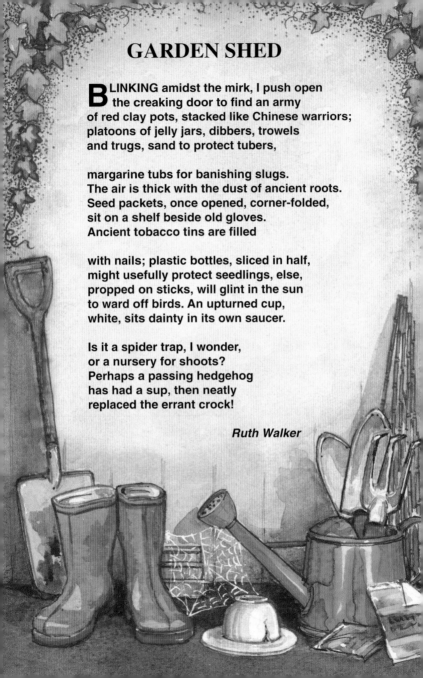

GARDEN SHED

BLINKING amidst the mirk, I push open
the creaking door to find an army
of red clay pots, stacked like Chinese warriors;
platoons of jelly jars, dibbers, trowels
and trugs, sand to protect tubers,

margarine tubs for banishing slugs.
The air is thick with the dust of ancient roots.
Seed packets, once opened, corner-folded,
sit on a shelf beside old gloves.
Ancient tobacco tins are filled

with nails; plastic bottles, sliced in half,
might usefully protect seedlings, else,
propped on sticks, will glint in the sun
to ward off birds. An upturned cup,
white, sits dainty in its own saucer.

Is it a spider trap, I wonder,
or a nursery for shoots?
Perhaps a passing hedgehog
has had a sup, then neatly
replaced the errant crock!

Ruth Walker

SEA FURY

I LOOK down from here,
from this daunting height,
my hilltop haunt, at where
the high tide cleaves
with long, relentless strokes,
and the sea-stressed rocks
are defiled by the bite
of headstrong waves;
at row upon ruinous row
of breakers, Armada-swelled

like wrecking galleons,
scuppered and quelled
on the salt-pied cliffs;
at a wild stampede
of skewbald stallions,
their frenzied hoofs
scattering sand and seaweed
as they rampage and riot,
thundering in and out
of the caves and coves below.

John Ellis

A TIME TO DREAM

DARK woods have called the beast to rest,
And skies with twinkling stars are dressed,
And all the mountain crests are calm
As if touched by an angel's palm:
A welcome hour for tawny owl,
Swift on the wing in silent prowl,
And pipistrelle in jerky flight,
The skilful hunters of the night.

A time to lend a listening ear
To hidden streamlets ringing clear
As breezy minstrels pluck their strings,
Light as a moth on gauzy wings:
A time to dream, a time to sense
The beauty in the ambience,
Whilst Phoebe, in her steady rise,
Makes quiet vales like paradise.

Alice Jean Don

CROCUS CUPS

MARCH gardens are wearing a Persian carpet of crocuses.
Tiny goblets of colour fused into tapestries
Of molten gold, purple and pearly-white.
Each Spring they pierce the grass with this glad spectacle.
Gold-stamened cups, undaunted by frosts or teasing winds.
A curving swathe of mingled shades,
Touching the passer-by with the delicate magic
Of Spring's recurring miracle.

Joan Howes

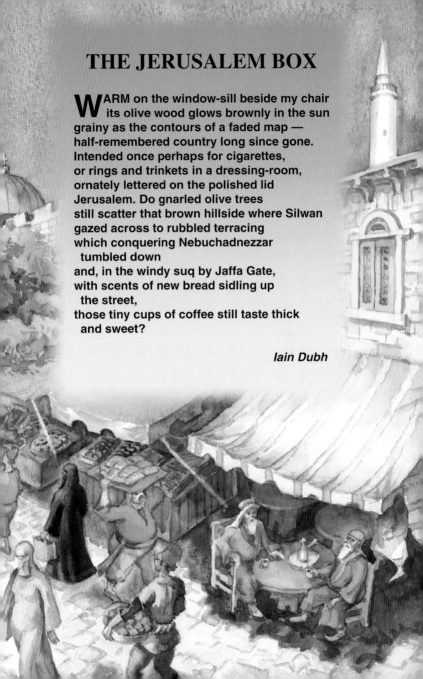

THE JERUSALEM BOX

WARM on the window-sill beside my chair
  its olive wood glows brownly in the sun
grainy as the contours of a faded map —
half-remembered country long since gone.
Intended once perhaps for cigarettes,
or rings and trinkets in a dressing-room,
ornately lettered on the polished lid
Jerusalem. Do gnarled olive trees
still scatter that brown hillside where Silwan
gazed across to rubbled terracing
which conquering Nebuchadnezzar
  tumbled down
and, in the windy suq by Jaffa Gate,
with scents of new bread sidling up
  the street,
those tiny cups of coffee still taste thick
  and sweet?

Iain Dubh

RECIPE

TAKE a plot of peaceful woodland,
  place beneath a gentle sky,
scatter with a dash of raindrops,
leave in sunshine till it's dry.
Take a billion bulbs of bluebells,
bury them in softest loam
Leave to rise till shining colour
floods the wood like drifting foam.
When their perfume sends you dizzy,
garnish with a blackbird's song,
serve upon a perfect morning,
savour all the Springtime long.

Margaret Ingall

WALLFLOWERS

I SETTLED you in Autumn
Lonely wallflowers,
Your tapered leaves
Slender and vigorous.
You weathered a weary Winter
Not seeking attention though,
Maybe unknown to you,
I gazed upon you many a day
When your fragrant loveliness
Seemed a million miles away.
Now you are here
Fulfilling an April morning;
Orange, yellow, and bronze
My patio adorning.
The crocuses have been,
The daffodils are gone,
So I will savour you
'til Springtime days are done.

Don Robinson

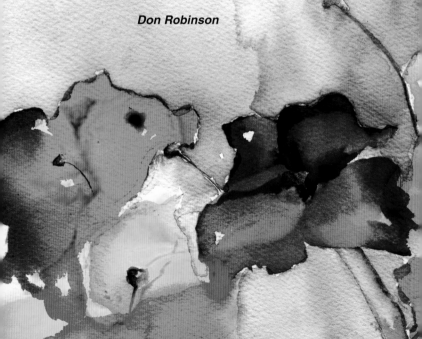

MAY DISPLAY

LABURNUM tassels hang in space,
 With awe-inspiring simple grace,
A yellow ochred pure bliss,
As gentle as a lover's kiss,
No other bloom could ever bring,
A better welcoming to Spring,
There is no tree I know possesses,
The equal of these golden tresses,
Small wonder in the month of May,
Our hearts rejoice at her display.

Brian H. Gent

FALLEN BRANCH

A SCAPULA of wood, I dragged you home,
Rinsed off the sea and sand, hosed you
Down to admire your hills and plains.

I allowed my hand to follow
Your flowing hollows, set you
Askew amongst the gravel.

Already you have proved to be
A hide for battalions of beetles,
My cats limber up to trim you

With their claws. They rub their fur
Against your denuded form. Soon,
Snow will cover you, creeping moss clings

Continually, until you return to ground
And feel the thud of breakers on the shore.

Ruth Walker

FAIRGROUND SKY

DAWN'S sky is a fairground attraction,
full of pulsing light,
colours that whirl and dance
like Waltzers in the breeze,
breath-stealing as a rollercoaster.

There's a backdrop,
painted purple as the Tarot tent,
that now flashed yellow and orange
as if the entire stock of goldfish has
    escaped.

The rock beat is replaced by birdsong,
but the enthusiasm is the same.
Even crows sound as if they're having
    a good time,
while seagulls wolf the candyfloss
    clouds.

Rowena M. Love

LUNAN BAY

IN places the sun shone munificently,
A brilliant white spotlight
Picking out a boat, a bit of shoreline,
Or the headland house
Perched high on cliff.

In places the Painted Ladies
Paraded themselves
On thistle tops and waste ground edge,
Treasure-troving pollen
Like hordes of gold dust.

In places the sand sang melodies
Sweet, soft, serene
Of a long, dry Summer
Sounding from beneath
Her bare white feet.

But everywhere the sea's rhythm
Floated free, constant and calming,
Flowing into us, as if intravenously,
It filled our blood with the nourishment
Of a day at Lunan Bay.

David Elder

LINNET

I HEARD a linnet through the trees,
jauntily, upon the breeze;
a joyous burst of gilded song
that pierced my heart, sweet and long,
and shivered on the air.

All fell still to hear the notes
that dipped and soared and seemed to float;
leaf and bough reached reverently,
grasses raised their heads to see
the psalm ascending there.

I know why angels leave their berth,
I know where Heaven kisses earth —
beyond the stand of low-limed larch,
beneath the forest's fragrant arch,
to bless the linnet fair.

Rachel Wallace-Oberle

RICH

EARLY sunlight on the path
coaxes me into the garden
where pure bullion of primrose,
jonquil, celandine and cowslip
gleam in Nature's almonry.

El Dorado's streets were never
metalled with such brilliance,
carat or luxuriance to compare
with this new-lit, dew-draped garden,
coffered in silver and gold.

Even the grass is sprayed with liquid
silver, and from every tree and bush
dawn's feathered tipsters, tick-tack
and trill the best of odds, with morning's
luminary hot favourite to win.

John Ellis

CLOUD SKY

ICEBERG clouds mass in a cornflower blue sky,
meringues curl into changing peaks
of froth and foam or lace edged shells
of rising dough. Grinning polar bears,
then hoary men slip past.
Now Neptune's beard,
there goes his trident spear,
All at once, Jason and his Golden Fleece
sweep by. Leda swoons, enraptured
by her swan.

Miniscule, sun trapped in Earth's embrace,
I sip my tea on a pocket handkerchief of lawn.

Ruth Walker

ECHOES

THE sun set sail today over continents.
Serene and rose and gold on the gun
metal sea. The saffron poppies and
seaweed. Joss-stick of Summer days.
The eagle-eyed seagull and honeysuckle
flower and collect bees. Sweet echoes.
The sun set sail today.

Dorothy McGregor

DREAMING

I'M lying in the Summer grass;
How slow the sleepy hours pass.
Drifting o'er the deep blue sky
A bird on lazy wings goes by.

Not the slightest breath of breeze
Stirs the silent, watchful trees.
On this enchanted day, it seems,
Summer brings me gentle dreams.

No one else to break the spell;
A dove calls softly from a dell.
Treasured moments, so sublime,
Conceal the onward march of time.

The distant hills, they call to say:
Though day's joys must pass away,
Night will bring her own sweet boon:
The magic of the rising moon.

Peter Cliffe

THE ROCK POOL

THERE is a little world down there,
  Warm and crystal clear,
Where countless little creatures live,
White horses they don't hear.
Nor do they dread the pounding hooves
That gallop on the shore.
Within those rocky recesses
Tranquillity is law.

Tiny shrimps dart to and fro
And send up puffs of sand;
A red anemone that waves
Its many-fingered hand,
And in a watery forest glade
Of fleshy weed and fern
Who knows what ocean tiger sleeps
And waits for tides to turn?

Don Robinson

BLISSFUL HOURS

FLITTING fleeting Summer days,
Basking in the sun's warm rays,
Daisy, dog-rose, buttercup,
Sweet nectar gladly offer up,
Who could deny,
A butterfly,
Her floral bower's,
Blissful hours . . .

Brian H. Gent

NORTH OF WOOLWICH

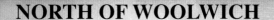

WHEN I see ice storms gather on the rim
   of churning, clotted skies turned outside in,
when asters kneel to supplicate the wind,
and birches arch their limbs and all but sing,
I await an undiminished thing.
For here, among the cosy lanes and streets,
and fields laid out like freshly laundered sheets,
where gentled woods commune in parcels neat,
Nature rarely stirs herself to mete
declarations lashed with ice and sleet.
But in her rising temper uncontrite,
that bends the lacquered trees from left to right,
broken glass, refracted by the light,
crystallises Heaven's shattered heights
and glazes every earthly thing in sight.

Rachel Wallace-Oberle

GARDEN COTTAGE

I MARK the contours with my pencil:
circular wall, crazy paving,
neo-Gothic windows smothered
with roses, chairs scattered
lazily in the sun.

White doves flutter round my head,
settle on the roof, puff and croon.
Crouched down, I become
part of the scenery. The bantam
cockerel stops rushing frantically,
keeps up a commentary by my side.

One black hen poses for my brush,
blinks her wrinkled eye. Skye,
the lurcher, noses past, sniffing
the stones. I place the date, carved
on the lintel: "Seventeen eighty one"
Bruising rosemary between my fingers

I pick out golds and pinks
to catch the blooms
before the night falls.

Ruth Walker

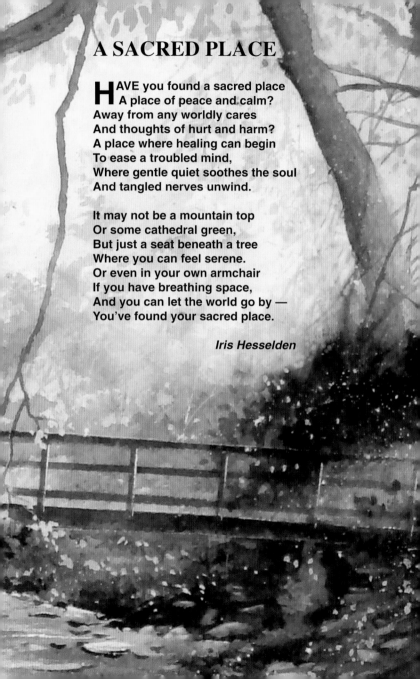

A SACRED PLACE

HAVE you found a sacred place
A place of peace and calm?
Away from any worldly cares
And thoughts of hurt and harm?
A place where healing can begin
To ease a troubled mind,
Where gentle quiet soothes the soul
And tangled nerves unwind.

It may not be a mountain top
Or some cathedral green,
But just a seat beneath a tree
Where you can feel serene.
Or even in your own armchair
If you have breathing space,
And you can let the world go by —
You've found your sacred place.

Iris Hesselden

TO BLOOM AGAIN

AN oasis in the wilderness
Once bereft of green
With spade and hoe and cooling rain
Will rainbow's garden gleam.
Whispers of magnolia
Of sweeter fragrance won
And trellis roses winding round
The heart of Summer spun.
Once a place of earthen clay
And dandelions spread
Now spills with magic, flowering seeds
Sewn with the sun's gold thread.

Dorothy McGregor

SOMETHING IN THE CITY

IF you are something in the city,
   confidently sitting pretty,
F.T. Index and Dow Jones,
checked each day on mobile phones.
Your quirky piles of stocks and shares,
fighting with the Bulls and Bears.
Should you buy or should you sell,
the trouble is no-one can tell.
So here's a tip I'll give to you,
a sound investment through and through.
Buy a pack of poppy seed,
no need to nurture or to feed.
The priceless dividend you'll yield,
are gems that make a poppy field.

Brian H. Gent

DANDELION DAYS

DANDELION, dandelion,
　　Won't you tell me true,
Where all the years have flown away
Since first your seeds I blew?
Since first I ran through meadow-grass
And days stretched long and free,
With dandelions the only clock
To tell the time for tea.
Yet do the days just disappear
Like seeds that drift away?
Or do they live forever on
In some mysterious way?
For still within me dwells that child
Who hears Truth's teasing call
That clocks are but a human toy
And time means naught at all.

Margaret Ingall

SNOOZIN'

LITTLE tabby pussy cat
　Lying in the sun
Gently, gently toasting
Till one side is done.
Languidly roll over
Re-arrange a paw
Flitter ears and whiskers
Go to sleep once more.
Deeply, deeply slumber
Rapt, in feline dream
Of fishy things and catnip mice
And saucers full of cream.
Let no care disturb you
Know, whate'er you crave
Will be laid before you
By this willing slave.
Epitome of furry grace
Embodiment of fun
Little tabby pussy cat
Lying in the sun.

Tricia Sturgeon

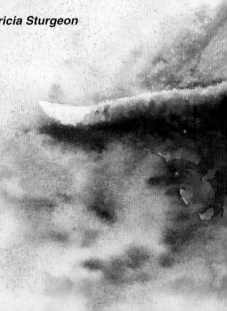

THE WELL

I FOUND a well once
In the dark green heart of a wood

Where pigeons ruffled up into a skylight of branches
And disappeared.

The well was old, so mossed and broken
It was almost a part of the wood

Gone back to nature. Carefully, almost fearfully,
I looked down into its depths

And saw the lip of water shifting and tilting
Heard the music of dripping stones.

I stretched down, cupped a deep handful
Out of the Winter darkness of its world

And drank. That water tasted of moss, of secrets,
Of ancient meetings, of laughter,

Of dark stone, of crystal —
It reached the roots of my being

Assuaged a whole Summer of thirst.
I have been wandering for that water ever since.

Kenneth Steven

WAKING

AS Spring shakes out her garments green and gold
and Winter abdicates its reign of cold,
my cottage by the water-lilied brook
begins to dream of blooms in every nook.

Upon the mantel scarlet poppies pose,
beside the door, a fragrant froth of rose,
on every table, freesia, bluebell, phlox
and hyacinth spill from the window box.
The porch envisions clouds of hollyhocks
that nod and bow to blushing four-o' clocks,
and all along the wall that faces west,
pansies primp, each costumed in their best.

Such rhapsodies that set the air aglow
and ornament the grasses! And then, oh!
Bewitchingly, among the perfumed hours,
Spring awakes my cottage with her flowers.

Rachel Wallace-Oberle

MAGIC TRACERY

WHITER than the whitest snow,
   Your chaliced blooms begin
  to show,
Tendrils tentatively twine,
By feverfew and columbine,
Down the lane and up the path,
You sign your special autograph,
Where in Summer would we be,
Without your magic tracery
Of verdant leaf and tender truss,
Bestowed by wild convolvulus.

Brian H. Gent

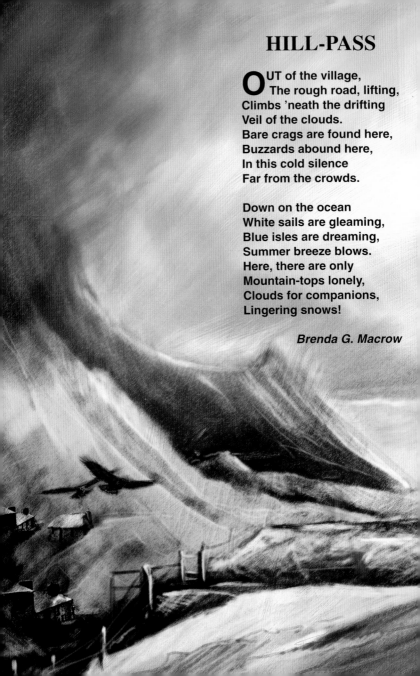

HILL-PASS

OUT of the village,
  The rough road, lifting,
Climbs 'neath the drifting
Veil of the clouds.
Bare crags are found here,
Buzzards abound here,
In this cold silence
Far from the crowds.

Down on the ocean
White sails are gleaming,
Blue isles are dreaming,
Summer breeze blows.
Here, there are only
Mountain-tops lonely,
Clouds for companions,
Lingering snows!

Brenda G. Macrow

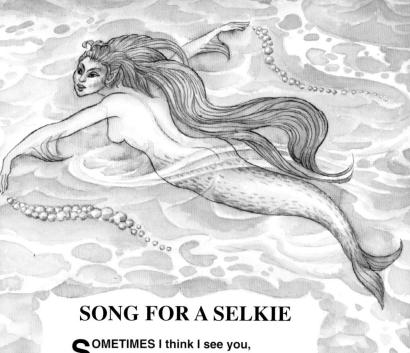

SONG FOR A SELKIE

SOMETIMES I think I see you,
sometimes I'm almost sure . . .
A movement in the water
where nothing was before.
Oh, will you come, my dear one,
to live once more with me,
and leave behind your sealskin
beside the restless sea?
Or have those windswept waters
reclaimed you evermore,
to leave me lost and longing
still waiting on the shore?
I would not keep you captive,
yet cruel it is to see
that while you live unfettered,
my heart will ne'er be free.

Margaret Ingall

SUMMER DANCE

SCARLET rose against the wall,
How gracefully your flowers fall,
Your velvet petals glowing soft,
Scatter perfume sweet aloft,
And when, long after Summer wanes
and shining hips all that remains,
Thoughts of you on colder days,
Bring visions of your bright displays,
Such magic mem'ries you inspire,
Of your Summer dance of fire . . .

Brian H. Gent

ONTARIO SUMMER

WHILE August hammered sheets of sky from gold
and lanced each limpid cloud with searing flame,
a cheerful summons through the heat cajoled;
I heard a red-winged blackbird call my name.

Loud and long from where he gaily perched
upon a fence that carried tangled wire,
the singer sang of tossing silver birch,
of winds that steepled into chilly spires,
of glades that brimmed with shy and silent shade.
I followed, bearing north, staying near;
on gleaming scarlet wing he nimbly bade
me to the Highlands where the air was clear.

There the lilac, pear
  and apple grow
and red-winged blackbirds
  gather to rejoice;
there among the scented hills
they know
Summer whispers in her sweetest
  voice.

Rachel Wallace-Oberle

SUMMERTIME'S END

WANING now the Summer heat,
  Preparing for that special treat,
When Autumn gold will cloak the land,
Where oak and ash and willow stand,
Chestnut's spiky fruit will drop,
And acorns from their cups will pop,
Swallows, swifts and martins too,
Will take their leave for pastures new,
Such are the fruits of Summer's labour,
Mellowed sweet for us to savour,
And 'neath a dark grey laden sky,
Winter will solidify,
As hoar frost stiffens tufts of grass,
And lakes and ponds become like glass,
Pale mists like gossamer will cling,
Until a bud turns green next Spring.

Brian H. Gent

EVENING IN AN ORCHARD

AS far as I can see along the fence,
   clinging like an ardent, blissful beau
to apple trees arranged with elegance,
mist crochets a sheer and lacy throw
and through the wild grasses ebbs and flows.

An early twilight dips across the trees
and pours the orchard full of dusky blue;
it seems as though expectant, noiseless leaves,
each silvered edge with opulence imbued,
are cast in moonlit filigree, renewed.

Is such enchantment just an earthly dream?
A fragile skein spun swiftly by the hours?
Among the low-limbed sentinels that seem
to genuflect within this hallowed bower
I stay, surrendered to a sacred power.

Rachel Wallace-Oberle

GOLDEN SEASON

TROVES of Autumn treasure and fruit
Of sweet chestnut burrs and blackberries,
mulberries and hip days. Wine to taste
and salad crisp at twilight's picnic.
The wind whistling thru' the trees and
on the high hills. Whisking the leaves of
russet gold. The old owl and wing bat
flitting the tree rafters. Bronzed with
October moonlight before the bright white
of Winter. And with Autumn's rekindling
fires. Gemlight and celebration.

Dorothy McGregor

INDIAN SUMMERS

MISTY morning, packing's done.
I leave my tears
where holy rivers run.
I leave my heart with you
when I am gone,
land of the Asian sun.

I will recall my Indian
Summers. Yet I wonder
if I shall ever see again
a greenness like your lush,
northern plain,
or a cloudburst like your monsoon rain.

Jasmine blossom, burning skies,
white, fantastic
marble palaces,
water straight from the well,
your almond eyes:
these are my memories.

John Ellis

CRAB-APPLE JELLY

SEPTEMBER.
MAKING it is fun:
slice, or quarter all,
this rosy-cheeked, acidic fruit
so round and small.
Brown-sugar it and simmer.
Sieve until you see
the amber almost-bitter syrup glimmer
clear and free
from skin to stem and pips.

DECEMBER.
Fires ablaze.
Short, dark, crackling,
roast-pork days.
We eat and talk
and yet
we quite forget
mouth-pursing Autumn-makings titillate
our jaded tongues and chapping Winter lips.

Not every yearned-for harvest
is sweetened by the sun.

REMEMBER.

Iain Dubh

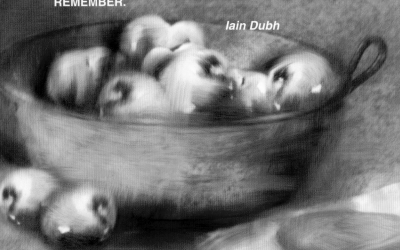

AUTUMN TOAST

GOLDEN morning pops into view.
It has a burnt crust where dawn
is singeing treetops amongst the trees
then settles as mist on neighbouring fields.

Nature's blade scrapes at the darkness
flecking crows against the light,
and a flock of cindered geese,
whose raucous call is the season's reveille.

Buttery cirrus is spread delicately,
ladylike, then cut on the diagonal
by a vapour trail.

In the east, with childish relish,
a spoonful of strawberry jam
oozes into the cumulus slathered there,
tinting everything pink.

Rowena M. Love

ANGEL OF THE NORTH

THE guardian Angel of the North,
  Watches citizens go forth,
In their cars and vans each day,
Beside the A1 Motorway,
Where men of grit and men of steel,
Wrought many a famous rugged keel,
And marched from Jarrow side by side,
From dawn until the eventide;
Now silent flows the River Tyne,
No engines clank nor hawsers whine,
No queues to form at dockyard gates
Or Geordie banter between mates;
Now too the pit heaps are grassed o'er,
Coal mining here exists no more,
No cages in the earth descend,
No weary miners homeward wend;
And so the legacy was sealed,
By wind-swept moor and lush green field,
By mountains high and sandy shore,
With oak and ash and sycamore,
So citizens can now go forth,
Watched by the Angel of the North . . .

Brian H. Gent

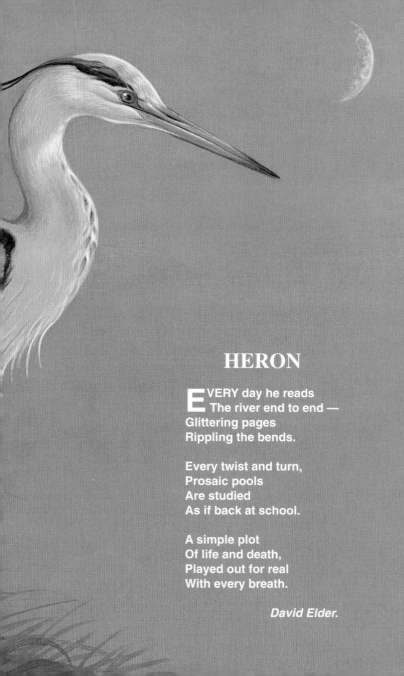

HERON

EVERY day he reads
The river end to end —
Glittering pages
Rippling the bends.

Every twist and turn,
Prosaic pools
Are studied
As if back at school.

A simple plot
Of life and death,
Played out for real
With every breath.

David Elder.

AUTUMN FLAMES

AS day tapers to a close,
 evening touches sun's sulphurous match
to beech, oak and birch already smouldering
with Autumn.

The freshening breeze swirls leaves,
fanning them to fall
in a flurry of sparks and ash,
soon doused in shadow.

Moments later, a downpour
hoses the trees, extinguishing all colour.
By the time the rain passes,
the glen is charred with night.

Rowena M. Love

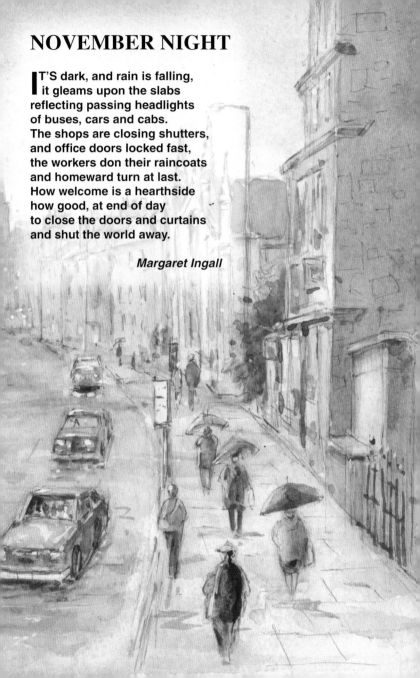

NOVEMBER NIGHT

IT'S dark, and rain is falling,
it gleams upon the slabs
reflecting passing headlights
of buses, cars and cabs.
The shops are closing shutters,
and office doors locked fast,
the workers don their raincoats
and homeward turn at last.
How welcome is a hearthside
how good, at end of day
to close the doors and curtains
and shut the world away.

Margaret Ingall

ADORNMENT

AT close of day, I pulled the heavy curtains,
And trod, with weary feet, upon each stair.
Whilst Winter's moonlight silvered starry heavens
Illuminating landscapes stark and bare.

When morning came, I drew apart the drapings
To find enchantment dancing in the air.
For gentle night had clothed the earth in diamonds
And dawn had tied pink ribbons in her hair.

Tricia Sturgeon

WINTER WEDDING

A GOWN as white as drifting snow,
   a veil as soft as mist,
a coronet like sparkling ice
by wintry sunlight kissed.
Her cheeks are pink, her eyes are bright,
her heart is beating fast,
inside the church her groom awaits,
their day has come at last!
Though snowflakes like confetti whirl
from silver skies above,
no Winter's blight could dim the light
of hearts aglow with love.

Margaret Ingall

SNOW-SCAPE

A FRAGILE hush of flakes, brushing the earth
As lightly as a diffident caress.
Softness more tenuous than drifting thoughts,
Harsh outlines blurred to phantom loveliness.

Petrified magic, movement held in thrall,
Tangible stillness pressed against the hills,
Casting blue shadows where the sleeping soil
Tenderly nurtures April's daffodils.

Joan Howes

The artists are:-

Matt Bain; Echoes,To Bloom Again.
Jackie Cartwright; Voice Of Spring,
Garden Shed, Linnet, Dreaming,
Golden Season.
John Dugan; The Jerusalem Box,
Cloud Sky, The Rock Pool, The Well,
Song For A Selkie.
Eunice Harvey; Fallen Branch,
Summer Dance.
Harry McGregor; April Frost,
Sea Fury, Lunan Bay,
Something In The City,
Summertime's End, November Night.
Keith Robson; North Of Woolwich,
Angel Of The North.
Maria Taylor; Evening In An Orchard.
Ruth M. L. Walker; January Blues,
Fairground Sky, Waking.
Joseph Watson; Winter Snows,
Crocus Cups, Blissful Hours,
Magic Tracery, Ontario Summer,
Heron.
Staff Artists; Falling Stars,
Song Thrush, Tread Softly,
A Time To Dream, Recipe, Wallflowers,
May Display, Rich, Garden Cottage,
A Sacred Place, Dandelion Days,
Snoozin', Hill-Pass, Indian Summers,
Crab-Apple Jelly, Autumn Toast,
Autumn Flames, Adornment,
Winter Wedding, Snow-Scape.